Dewey Decimal System Defeats Truman!

Dewey Decimal System Defeats Truman!

Library Cartoons

by
Scott McCullar

McFarland & Company, Inc., Publishers
Jefferson, North Carolina and London

British Library Cataloguing-in-Publication data are available

Library of Congress Cataloguing-in-Publication Data

McCullar, Scott.
    Dewey Decimal System defeats Truman! : library cartoons / by Scott
McCullar.
      p.   cm.
     ISBN 0-7864-0521-X (sewn softcover : 55# alkaline paper)
     1. Libraries — Caricatures and cartoons. 2. American wit and
humor, Pictorial. I. Title.
    NC1429.M4744A4   1998
    741.5'973 — dc21   98-13548
                                                    CIP

Manufactured in the United States of America

McFarland & Company, Inc., Publishers
  Box 611, Jefferson, North Carolina 28640

"*Love* is that condition in which the happiness of another person is essential to your own."
Robert Heinlein
Stranger in a Strange Land

═══════════════

To my champion

Nancy

friend

lover

wife

This romance has only begun.

Acknowledgments

To parents Alcie & Mike for raising a cartoonist full of delight, and to sister Lisa, brother Matt, and in-laws Betty & Tom.

For laugh support from friends Martha & Troyce, Steve & Laura, Rory, Bill, John, John-Tim & Cathy, Kim, Tom, Lynn, and Bobbie.

To fellow cartoonist Kevin Thomas for years of swapping ideas, and for his leftover press dots!

To the Texas A&M University newspaper, *The Battalion*, for years of cartooning support, and for its habit of publishing its own cartoonists.

For the kindness of the people in my library worlds: Texas A&M: Hal Hall, Mel Dodd, Candy Benefiel, Amy Shannon, Nan Butkovich; Harris County Public Library (Houston): Betty Ozbun, Karen Blankenship, Elaine Plotkin, Paul Bump, Rhoda Goldberg, Neil Campbell, David Jones, Bill Jarvis, Don Thomas, Mary Sommerfeld and *all* of the Children's Librarians.

And to "B.C." cartoonist, Johnny Hart, because...
"Clams got LEGS!"

A version of "...another word for synonym" appeared in *American Libraries*, November 1983 page 670, and in *The Bibliographic Instruction-Course Handbook* by Helen Rippier Wheeler, Scarecrow Press, Inc., 1988, page 116.

"After 70 hours of microfiche research..." appeared in *The Wilson Library Bulletin*, December 1993, page 84.

A version of "Libraries in space" appeared in the Vernon Library Supplies, Inc. publication *Tech-Note-Tips*, Fall 1994.

"Libraries in space…" appeared in *The Wilson Library Bulletin*, May 1995, page 80, as did "Library books sometimes like to check the patrons out." "Something very weird…" appeared in *American Libraries*, February 1996, page 67.

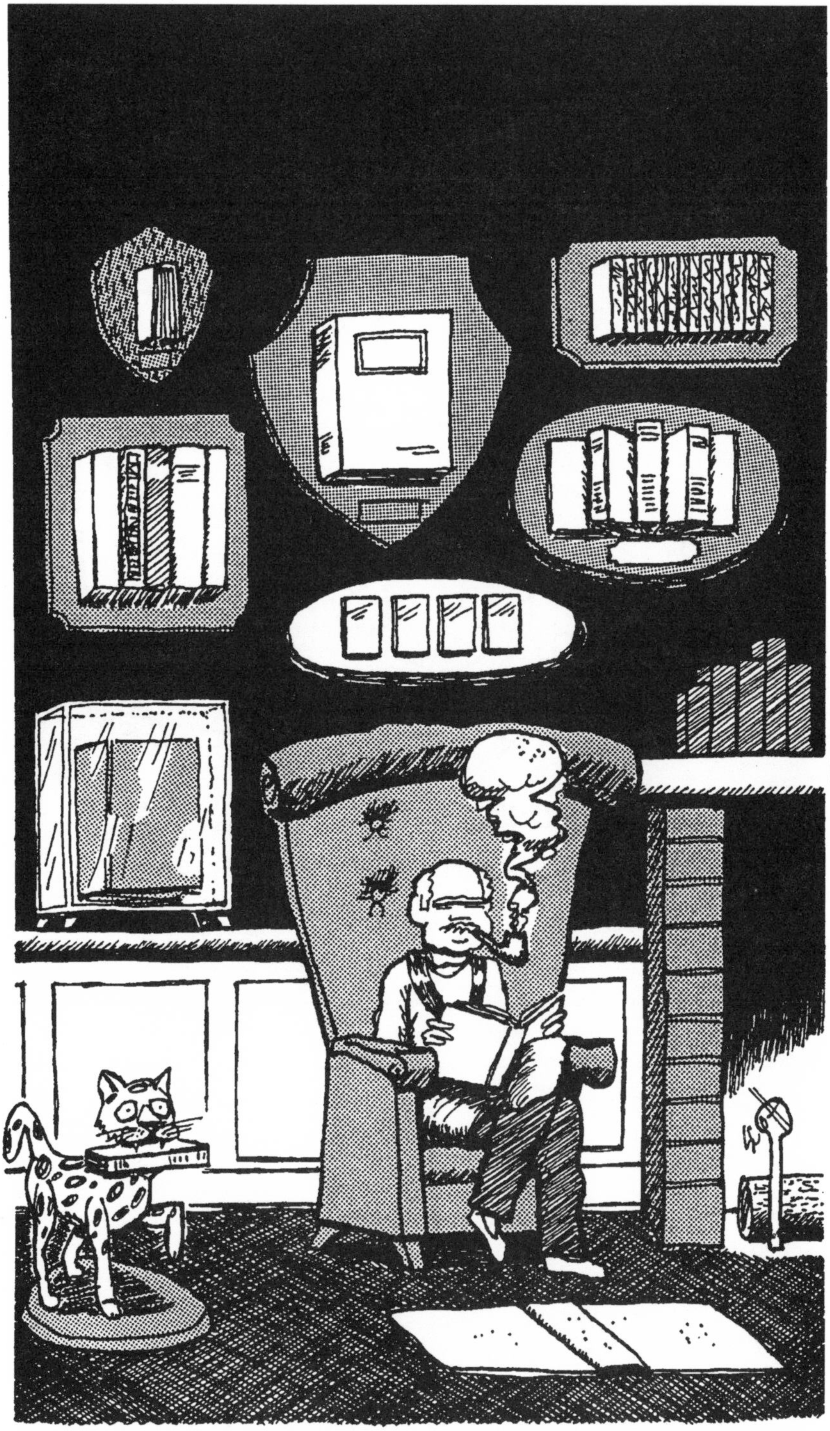

"Excuse me, I'm looking for a particular book I used once, but the keyword search 'blue cover' doesn't call it up."

"*O-O-O-O*, the judges didn't think much of *that* question. *Low* scores for the fact that he wanted the answer to a *class-assigned* research question, and that he waited till the last minute."

If you want a *really* quiet place to read, try the Mime Library.

The library didn't bother with censorship, but
did occasionally *spray* the books for indecency.

Libraries in space have a problem with the books "circulating."

The head of the Microtext Department at breakfast with his wife.

Nancy was the kind of reader that books themselves sought out.

Gretchen had worked the Reference Desk *way* too many
hours this week and couldn't *stop* providing information now.

Scratch Paper
Now on
CD-ROM

"Well, I give up. What *is* another word for synonym?"

"Well, I'm certainly glad
that new filthy exposé
bestseller isn't in *my* library…"

"…um, is it available
on Interlibrary Loan?"

"Nope, sorry. Can't help you.
I'm not a librarian, but I play one on TV."

Coming Soon To A Theater Near You

Alfred Paperback's

THE BOOKS

Wherever he ran, they collected around him...

Directed by Alfred Paperback

Read	READING STRONGLY RECOMMENDED
Some Material May Be Appropriate for Children Under 13	

You never get to provide the information you *know* they need.

Oh, sure, it's tough at *your* Reference desk.
Well, all we had was a *trench*. And when it rained it
filled with *water* and bred mosquitoes and tadpoles, and…

Librarians aren't any better at Trivial Pursuit than other people, they just know what shelves have the answers.

As a last resort you can always pull the "stuck-open
air freshener" trick on patrons who don't bathe.

A FEW LIBRARY BUDGET-CUT MEASURES

"O-O-O-kay," thought Mike, "no putting it off any longer.
I'm going to have to learn the online catalog."

23

"If you've come up with another new and completely different information storage format, we're going to have to skin you."

BOOKS OF THE WILD-PROTECTION & MANAGEMENT

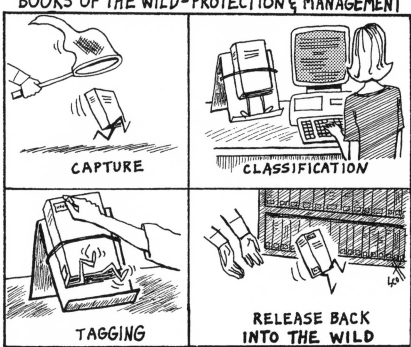

CAPTURE

CLASSIFICATION

TAGGING

RELEASE BACK INTO THE WILD

THE U.S.S. LIBRARIANSHIP
DIGNITY AT LOW PAY

Library Audiovisual Equipment User's Guide
Tip #27: the difference between Earphones and Headphones

EARPHONES

HEADPHONES

"He's not in his office at the moment.
Let me go online and see if he's in the bathroom."

No, Allen was right. When she'd asked him to shift the stacks she hadn't said *anything* about putting the books back with the spines facing out.

Betty returned to the library Microtext Department she'd used as a girl, but somehow everything seemed smaller than she remembered it.

"Hey, you *yahoo*, hurry it up with the book covers! We're freezing our card pockets off back here."

Without thinking Bill tore out the page
he wanted and learned an important lesson.

The ants had discovered the microfiche collection.
The knowledge there was the ideal size for them to use,
and their civilization evolved astronomically.

When Steve checked out Volume One,
the other twelve insisted on coming along.

The novelization of "ALIEN" had been waiting ...
waiting ... *waiting* for someone to flip through it.

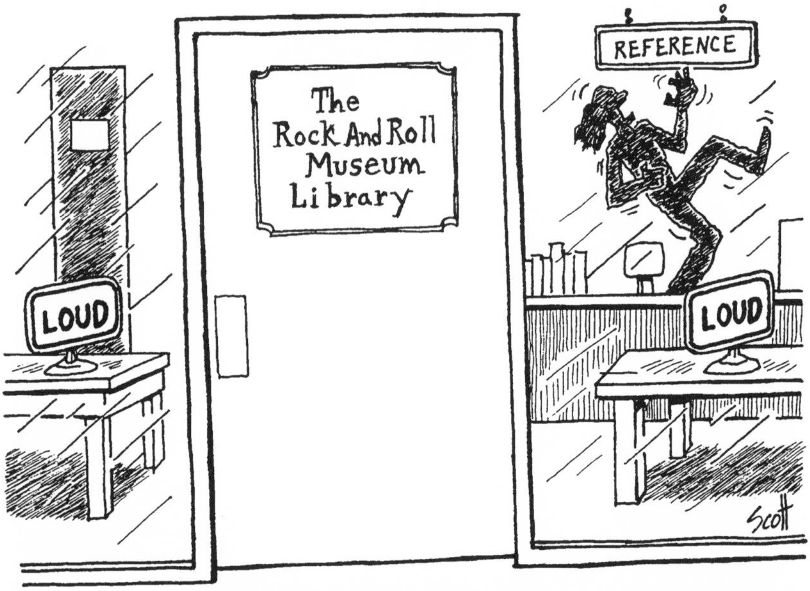
The Rock And Roll Museum Library
REFERENCE
LOUD
LOUD
Scott

30

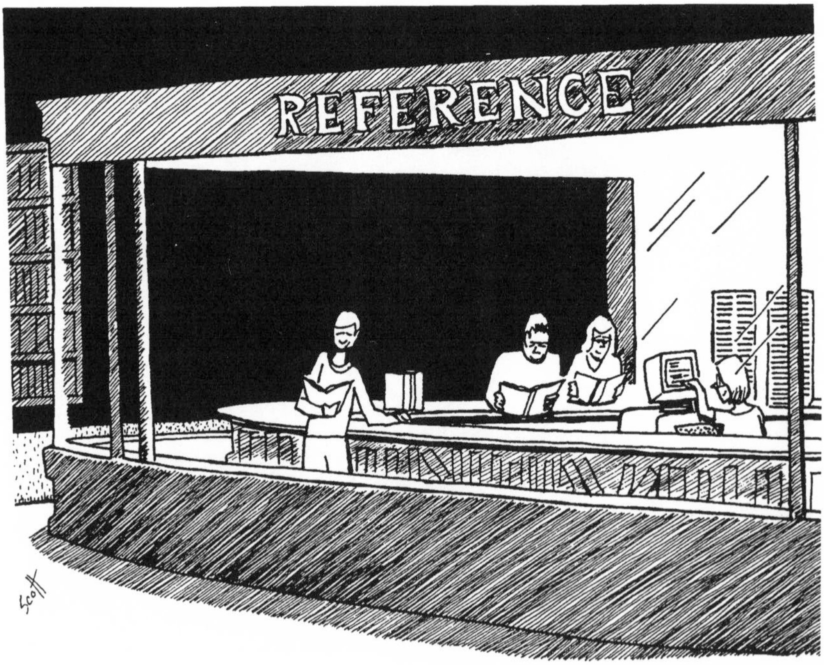
REFERENCE
Scott

"For God's *sake*, you've *got* to have smaller stick-on
notes on the supplies contract than the Super-Colossal size!"

"Hey, who stole all the cover?"

Branch Librarian Karen didn't know she had spare staff in storage.

He never got the LC system either.

"Sorry, fella. You know too much, you have to be killed."

On the great western book drives they
took the herds to libraries back east.

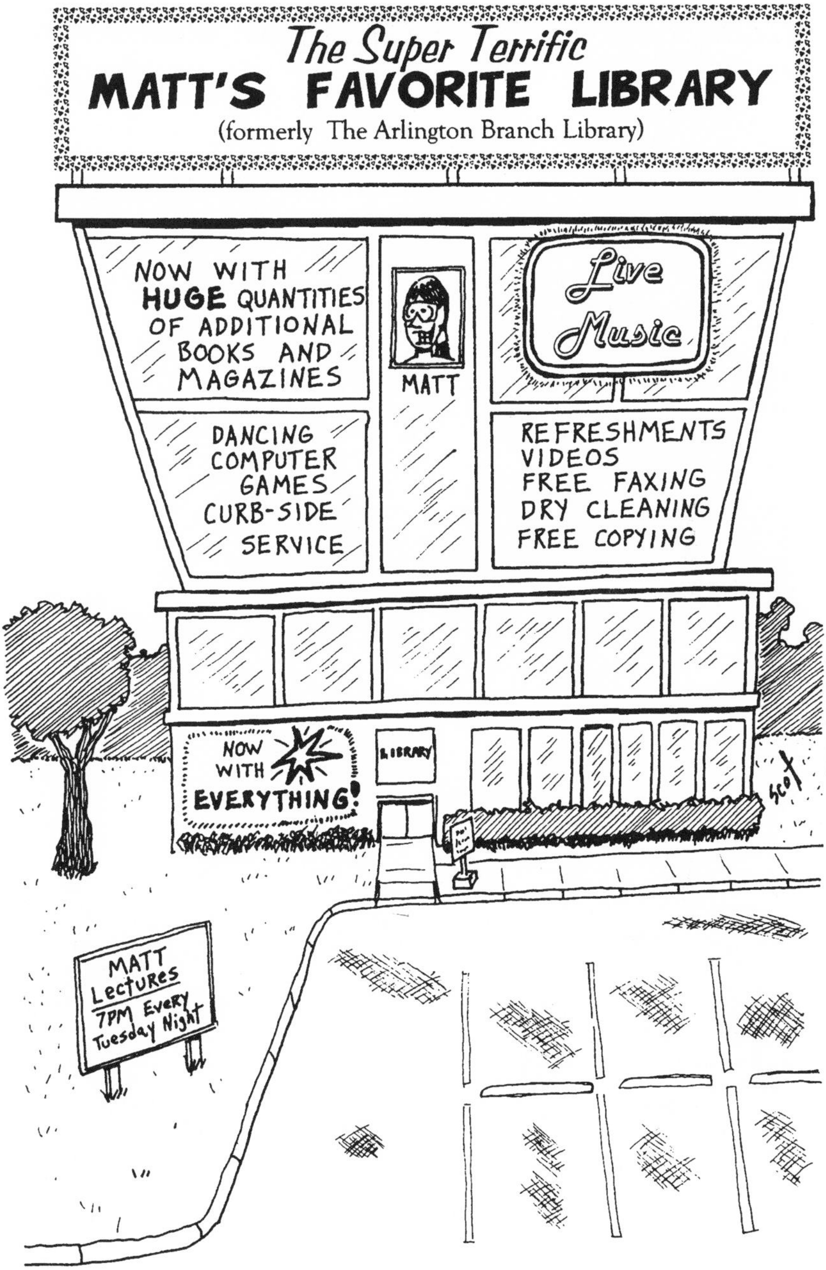

The Super Terrific
MATT'S FAVORITE LIBRARY
(formerly The Arlington Branch Library)
NOW WITH HUGE QUANTITIES OF ADDITIONAL BOOKS AND MAGAZINES
MATT
Live Music
DANCING
COMPUTER GAMES
CURB-SIDE SERVICE
REFRESHMENTS
VIDEOS
FREE FAXING
DRY CLEANING
FREE COPYING
NOW WITH EVERYTHING!
LIBRARY
MATT Lectures 7PM Every Tuesday Night

Don't judge them too harshly. They had *pitiful* funding before wealthy Friend-of-the-Library Matt came along.

For some reason the Mysto posters got more people reading than all the other celebrity posters combined.

A scene from the TV drama series "L.A. Library."

A disguise won't help. They can *sense* you're a librarian.

When reference books get "press-the-button"
sound effects chips like children's books.

A BOYHOOD DREAM COMES TRUE

At night the library books themselves used the computer
terminals to find and meet other interesting books.

REFERENCE

Rumor was that the "Q" volume of the encyclopedia was
a *banned book*, so naturally patrons wanted it like crazy.

41

"Hello, 3rd floor? Your compact
shelving is making a run for it again!"

"You say it had a *white* cover? As big and white as a mountain of snow?"

"The Adventures of Huckleberry Finn" was
offended by Kevin and wouldn't let him read it.

After 73 hours of microfiche research, Hal learns the awful truth.

The library was *definitely* in need of more space after THE book arrived.

Library books sometimes like to check out the *patrons*.

Well … it's not *exactly* a rule, but if you want tenure in *this* campus library you wear the uniform and the hat.

First there were plastic covers on books and magazines
to protect and extend their lifespan. Then the
library's health insurance provider got into the act.

Library
Lass

Catalog
Kid

BookMan

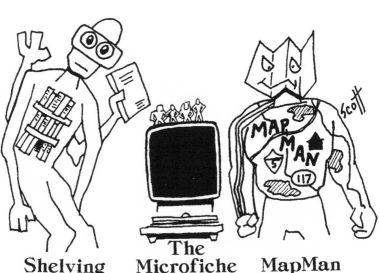

Shelving
Savior

The
Microfiche
Four

MapMan

Internet Ingenue

Captain Circ

Sir Serial

VILLAINS

Rip-Tear

Copier Killer

STAPLE

Vendor Villain

Budget Basher

scott

48

"Yeah, this is the one with the release problem all right."

"I've *done* it. I've figured out a way to put *spine labels* on CD-ROMS."

Another appearance of the Lost Library Tour of 1955.

John was new at the library and thought they
were keeping statistics for *dork* count week.

"No, it's not a hardware problem.
Looks more like a *soft*ware problem to me."

The library director at work.

"Hi, there. I have a high school term paper due tomorrow. Where do you keep them?"

"In accordance with the council's recent instruction to drastically reduce the library's budget ... we've had it put on microfiche."

Believe it or not, in this case the
book was *much* worse than the movie.

There are really only *two* types of patrons,
and libraries that truly want to meet the needs of
both have rolls that hang from the front *and* the back.

"There, see, I *told* you. You died in 1857. It says so right there!"

"The bad news is your CD-ROM drive has to be sent out for repair. The *good* news is I can loan you this ViewMaster to read them till it's fixed."

Tom likes commands.

"*There* you are. I've been waiting at this call number for over an *hour!*"

"Oh, I found that important "data-disk" thingy you were looking for and stuck it on your filing cabinet."

The new Elvis compact disc collection is an
audiovisual cataloger's nightmare, because it's a
kit that comes with a Giant-Size Box-O-Chicken dinner.

In the library at ancient Alexandria the scribes corrected small mistakes in the scrolls with Liquid Papyrus.

"Uh, we're just taking a *short* break."

Frontiersmen used to trap and skin books
and wear their pelts for warmth.

Maybe the only way to keep periodicals safe while they're
being read: locked inside laboratory-safe glove boxes.

"My goodness, everyone's looking for books about *reptiles* all of a sudden. I wonder if there's a big school assignment."

If a book starts getting boring Martha gives it a really *good*
shaking until some interesting parts come to the surface.

The new perfumed inter-office mailing envelopes really kept the mail *moving* through the library.

Even library TV talk show hosts have the same old problems.

When moms work the reference desk.

Another insurance salesman finds the books on mind control.

You can't afford any slow spots in a children's librarians' meeting. These people make craft projects if they get bored.

"Ah, here's the answer. The book you want isn't checked out, it's just on vacation for two weeks."

"I'd like a word with you about all the titles I've
discovered in the catalog under the 'Earl' classification."

"Morning, professor. The library doesn't own
the book you assigned your classes to read there. They said
there's *lots* of copies buried in your front yard, though."

You've got to *hand* it to people who can describe things over the phone.

70

"Ma'am, do you have any 'Magic Eye' 3-D books on audiotape?"

Martha Stewart Library

Libraries probably shouldn't even purchase mystery novel pop-up books.

"Send a fire truck to the library, *quick*! A patron opened *all* of the cologne flaps in a *Vogue* and a *Cosmopolitan*!"

Super Model
Vendela

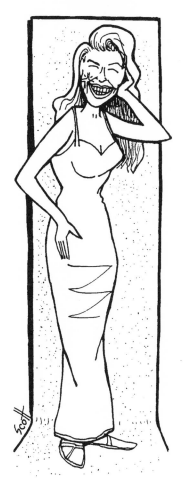

Super Librarian
Nancy

"Administration? The security gates are shorting
out and functioning like time portals again."

"Oh, no ... not your Elton John impersonation again."

Middle of the night UFO book abduction:
the mystery of lost library books explained?

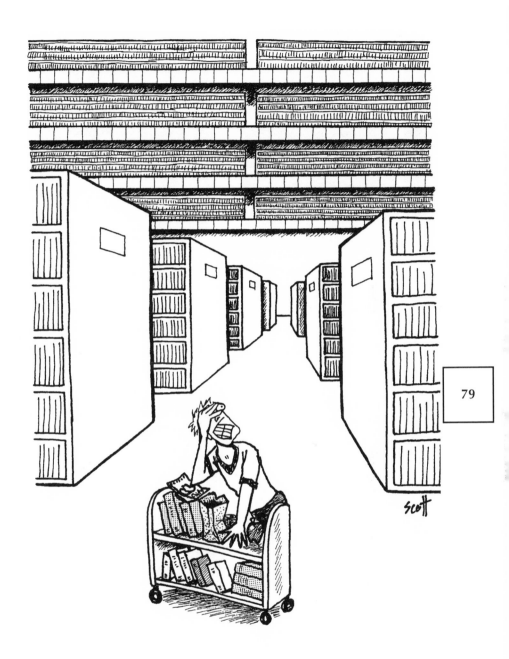

Allen realizes that *somewhere* he's
shelved both of his tuna fish sandwiches.

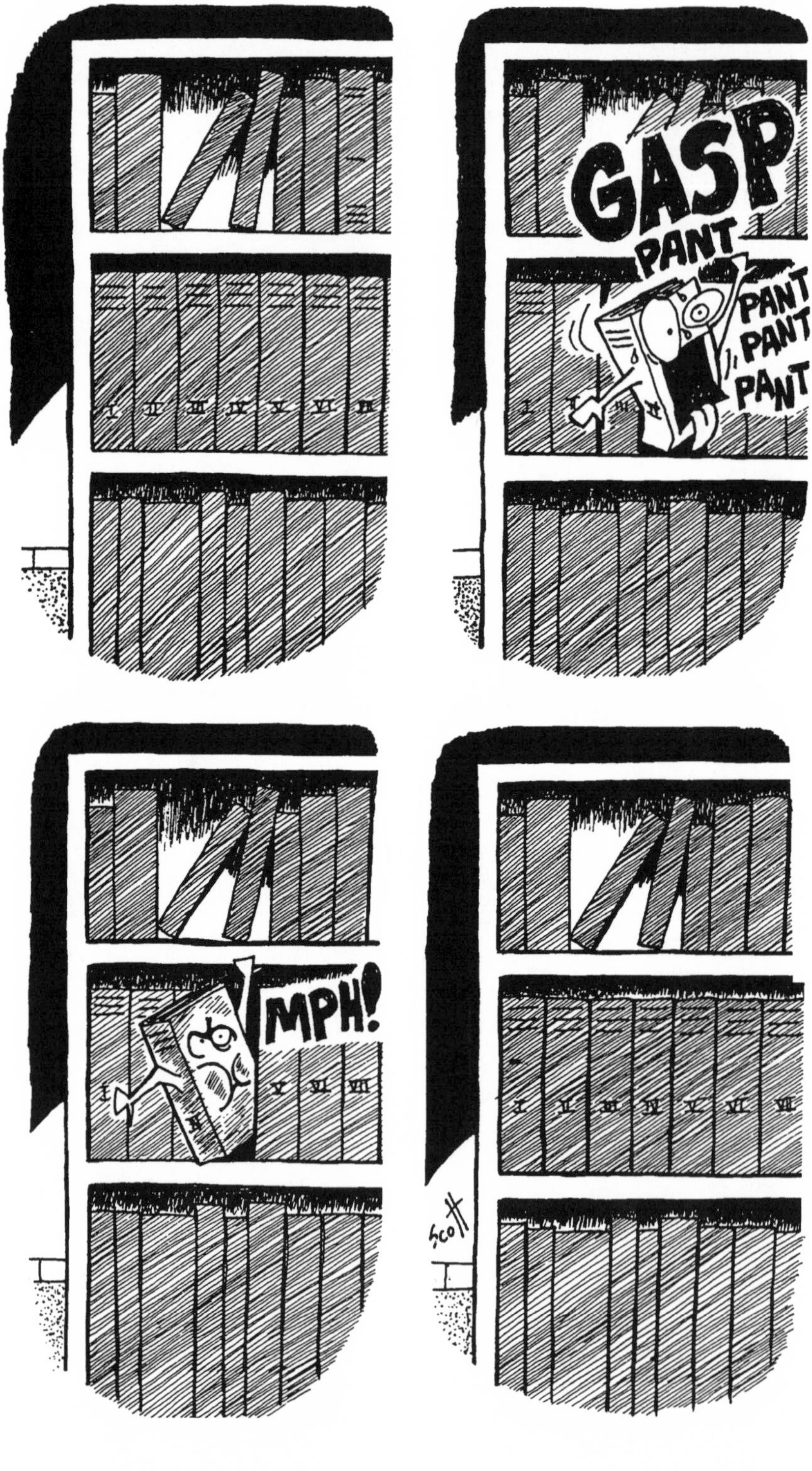
GASP
PANT
PANT
PANT
PANT
MPH!

A collection preservation method
in previous centuries—books in alcohol.

"C'mon, you, tell us what we want to know!
We've got a bib record on you as long as my arm!"

Librarians on steroids.

"Yes, hello. I need to get some details about one of the books
you publish. It's the really crappy one, the one that's an
embarrassment to the entire publishing industry … I was wondering
why you published it and why it's so damned expensive?"

**Reference On the Move: Daryl likes the freedom
to wander the building helping patrons.**

"You're *obviously* looking for the microfiche readers."

It's really too bad library workers don't get to pose in triumph after performing routines the way ice skaters do.

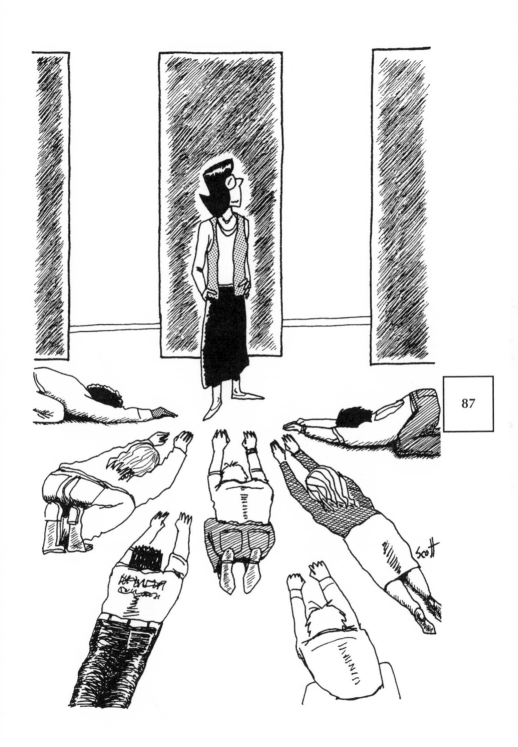

She Who Knows Where Info Lives

If a book is open in the forest, does anyone read it?

"Something very *weird* has happened to this checkout wand."

"You always thought you were *better* than me, didn't you? I was never *good* enough for you and your smug, *hands-on* format."

Oh, sure, zombies make cheap, tireless, 24-hour-a-day
shelvers, but they still can't put the books in right side up.

The Library Psychic-Friends Network finds the hidden truth again.

Mercenary librarians.

A scene from John Grisham's work-in-progress, "The Library."

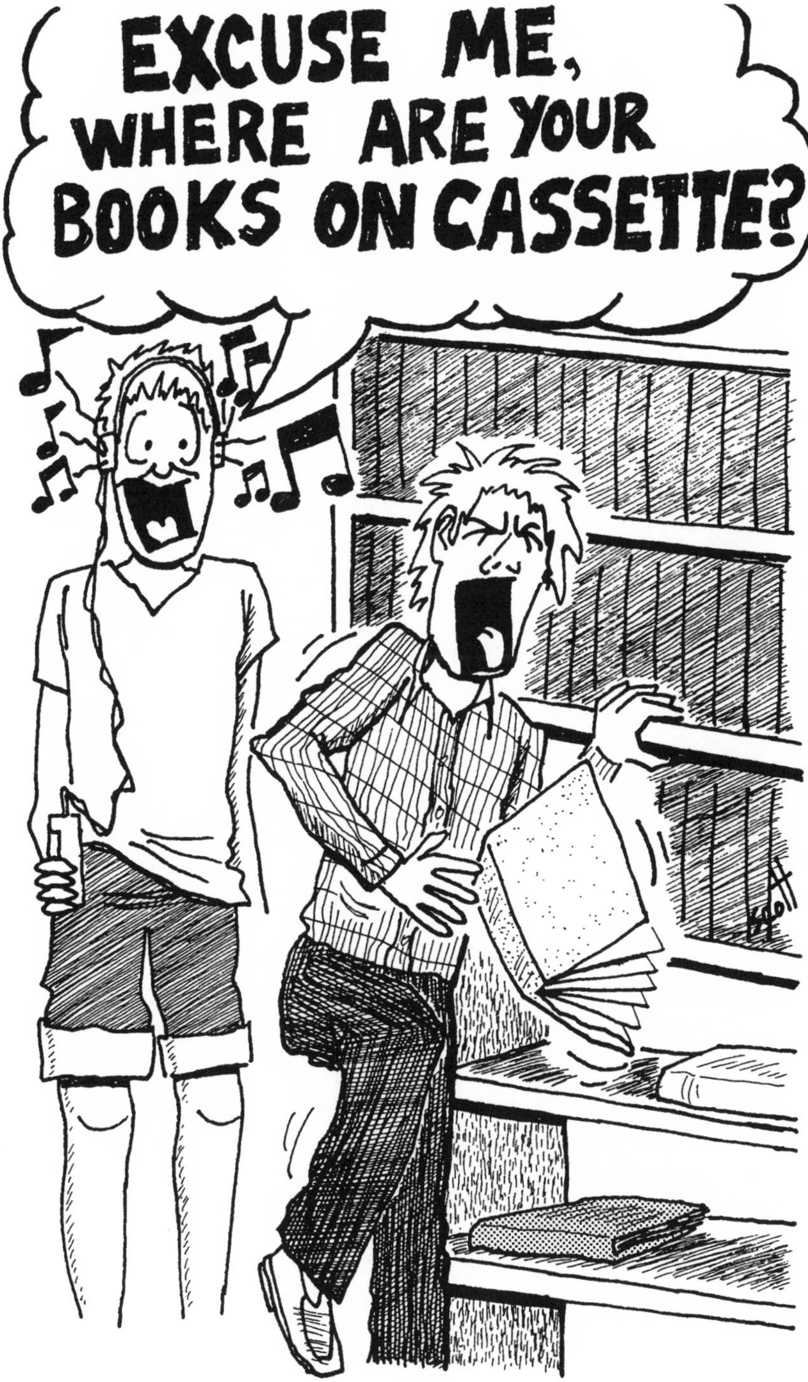
EXCUSE ME, WHERE ARE YOUR BOOKS ON CASSETTE?

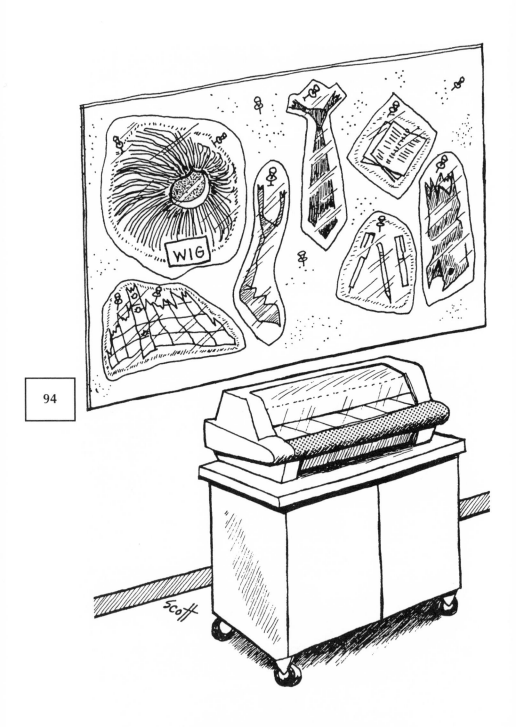

The library's "I-Bent-Too-Far
Over-the-Lamination-Machine" collection.

READ

In space no one can hear you read.

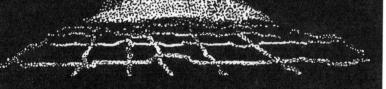

Scott